SIX DAYS TO
SATURDAY

———————

JOE PATERNO
AND PENN STATE

JACK NEWCOMBE

SIX DAYS TO SATURDAY

JOE PATERNO AND PENN STATE

PHOTOGRAPHS BY DICK SWANSON

FARRAR, STRAUS AND GIROUX

NEW YORK

FIRST PRINTING, 1974

PRINTED IN THE UNITED STATES OF AMERICA

PUBLISHED SIMULTANEOUSLY IN CANADA BY

DOUBLEDAY CANADA LTD., TORONTO

DESIGNED BY CYNTHIA KRUPAT

Library of Congress Cataloging in Publication Data

Newcombe, Jack.

Six days to Saturday: Joe Paterno and Penn State.

1. Pennsylvania. State University—Football—Juvenile literature.

2. Paterno, Joe—Juvenile literature.

3. Football—Juvenile literature.

4. Football coaching—Juvenile literature.

[1. Paterno, Joe.   2. Football coaching.   3. Football]   I. Title.

GV958.P46N48   796.33′263′0974853   74–11207

ISBN 0–374–36975–5

CONTENTS

We work hard to achieve our goals and when Saturday comes and we walk on the grass in the stadium, we stand as a team. We tighten up our belts. We look across at our opponents. We say, "Come on. Let's go. Let's see how good you are. Let's play." We are ready. We play with enthusiasm and recklessness. We aren't afraid to lose. If we win, great, wonderful—and the alumni are happy for another week. But win or lose, it is the competition that gives us pleasure.

It is being involved in a common cause which brings us joy and memories which endure in teammates.

It is making our very best effort, that we have stretched to the very limit of our ability, which makes us bigger men and more able to stretch again: to reach even higher as we undertake new challenges.

FROM THE COMMENCEMENT ADDRESS
AT PENNSYLVANIA STATE UNIVERSITY, 1973,
BY JOE PATERNO

1|SUNDAY AT THE MOVIES

IN THE small windowless room the broken whirring sound of the movie projector cuts into the Sunday-morning silence of the gymnasium. The hurrying figures on the screen run forward and then dance backward, like some old comedy movie, as the projector repeats each play three times. There are seven men sitting around the table looking up intently at the screen. Occasionally they make quick notes on the legal pads in front of them. It is the beginning of another work week for the football coaching staff at Pennsylvania State University. It is a week that seems to have a beginning but no real ending.

The coaches are taking a long look back at the game played by Penn State less than twenty-four hours before. For Head Coach Joe Paterno and three of his assistants who were on the field with the team on Saturday, it is their first chance to see what really happened in the game. At ground level, where there is a constant shuttle of players, managers, officials, the coaches sense what is going on but miss many of the details of the action. The coaches who were spotting in the press box—and the movie camera—have recorded the real reasons for the team's successes and failures in the game.

At the Sunday-morning meeting Coach Paterno and his assistants are both critics and rooters. It is the one meeting in the coaches' offices when they work without wearing ties and without interruption, and look at last week's results before plunging into preparations for the next game. The film has been processed overnight for this early Sunday showing. A copy of it, or one similar to it, will soon be in the hands of Penn State's next opponent. Most universities cooperate with one another in the exchange of game films.

On the screen the visitors' first-period touchdown is run over and over again. A Penn State defensive safety made a mental error on his assignment, failing to protect his ground, and the quarterback raced around him for a score. Paterno is almost as angry as he was on the field watching one player's lack of concentration hurt the team. "A big-league goal-line stand ruined!" he exclaims. No one speaks as the camera shows the scoreboard clock and the first-period score of 14–7 in favor of Penn State. Moments later State's defensive halfback drops the quarterback for a loss.

"That's the 8 Blow!" says one of the assistants, pleased that the carefully rehearsed rush of the quarterback had worked perfectly.

"Don't slow down, don't slow down when you're free!" Paterno yells at the screen as he watches a Penn State end run a pass pattern.

A long field goal by the opponents of over fifty yards brings praise from the coaches. "You could really hear him hit that," one of them exclaims.

Another Penn State touchdown, on a long run that had brought a crowd of over 50,000 to its feet on Saturday, fails to impress the coaches. "They're not tackling very well, are they?" an assistant comments. To the fans it had looked like a super effort by the ball carrier and his blockers. The coaches could see that the touchdown had come too easily.

The kickoff by Penn State causes more concern. The visitors run the ball back to good field position. "Look at the left side!" an assistant says. "They're knocking us down." He asks to see it again; the kick-off is rerun for the fourth time. The coaches carefully study the coverage and the blocks that had given the ball carrier so much running room.

The game action is interrupted as an injured Penn State player is helped to the sidelines. "How is it?" a coach asks. "He took a shoulder in the knee after he caught the pass," Paterno says.

They learn more about the injury within a few moments when an assistant coach, who has been making the check at the training quarters several blocks away, brings in the Sunday medical report. The advice from the team physician and the trainer can be bad news or not so bad news. Some injuries that appear to be serious on the sidelines on Saturday turn out to be minor when they are examined on Sunday. Other bruises and pains develop into handicaps overnight.

On this Sunday the news is not so bad: The knee injury to the end was more painful than serious. He should be at full speed soon. The offensive tackle, who has been on crutches with a badly bruised foot for several days, may be allowed to do "a little work" later in the week. An offensive guard and one of the linebackers are "red cross." They can report to practice on Monday but are not in shape to work out. They will watch from the sidelines wearing white shirts with a large red cross. It means they are to stay away from all contact. The injury list is short. The coaches will have to make only a few changes when they go to work with their offensive and defensive teams on Monday.

The third reel flashes on the screen with the start of the second half.

On Saturday, as Penn State was about to leave the locker room after halftime, Coach Paterno had encouraged his offensive co-captain, "Take the ball and knock it in." The team had done just that, scoring a touchdown within a few minutes. But quick, easy scores do not please coaches much. They are valuable to have on the scoreboard but they can lower the level of a team's performance. Watching the second-half action on the screen, Coach Paterno says to his assistants, "You can't see it from upstairs, but we were flat. There's no zoom."

The recording of mistakes and problems continues on the coaches' note pads. The assistant responsible for the offensive linemen carefully watches their blocking on a play called Pass 31. The assistant who coaches the quarterbacks sees the pass play fail as the ball is thrown away from the route run by the receiver. He exclaims, "Where's he throwing it!" Tomorrow, before the pass is tried in practice, he and the quarterback will talk about the throwing error.

As the third quarter sputters to an end, Coach Paterno says he's going home. He is anxious to get on with the planning for the next game. In the privacy of his study he will look at two or three reels showing the opponents in other games. He already knows what he wants to emphasize early in the week. Here, late in the season, the team's performance has flattened out. Neither coaches nor players were ready for the option play skillfully handled. Familiar assignments are being done routinely. Players and coaches need a jolt.

This early-afternoon break from the office also gives him time for a short nap before meeting with the staff and team later. Sunday is always a long day because he can never sleep the night after a game. As he heads out of the office for his car, he notes the stack of letters he has signed earlier, waiting for the secretary to mail in the morning. The letters offer congratulations to high school coaches in the state whose teams have done well in their conferences. They tell coaches:

"We are sure we are interested in some of the boys on your fine team and look forward to contacting them." The letters are another reminder that the coach must always look ahead. To next week's game. To next year. To the players he will want to see at Penn State several seasons from now.

F O R   M O S T of the eighty-man squad at Penn State, Sunday is a day of unwinding from the mental tensions and physical stiffness of the game. Sunday is a day to "sleep in" at the dormitories, fraternity houses, and apartments where they stay. It's a day to return to the books they haven't touched since Friday. A day without football—except for the pro games they will probably watch on TV and the film meeting they must attend in the evening. Unlike many universities, Penn States does not have a "football dorm" where all the players are housed. Coach Paterno wants the players to spend as much time as possible in the normal patterns of student life. He believes that teamwork and a sense of togetherness do not require players to live in isolation in a special dormitory.

The players have much more than football on their minds at this point in the season. They will be facing semester exams in the next two weeks. Despite the time they devote to football, most of them do better in the classroom than the average student at Penn State. Their choice in studies is as wide as the University itself. On this Sunday the team's place kicker is concentrating on biology, his major. One of the married players is doing work for an education course on exceptional children. A defensive back and a second-team center are both trying to keep up with premedical studies. At the fraternity house where he is president, the team's offensive co-captain studies to keep his grades up and stay on the Dean's List. A fullback wrestles with the details of his course in corporate finance. A defensive back flips through the pages of his German reader, preparing for a Monday-morning exam. On Saturday he had found that German vocabulary and thoughts about the game were both on his mind. He knows he didn't play as well as he should have. Now he wonders how he will do on the German test in the morning.

The Sunday-night squad meeting starts at 7:15 in the training quarters next to the practice fields. The players begin to arrive by car in small groups well ahead of the meeting time. Nearly every move they make during the week of practice is regulated by careful timing. They are expected to be on time for Sunday's meeting, just as they are expected to be lined up in time for Saturday's kickoff.

The training quarters are in a low brick building at the edge of the campus. It holds what a major university football team needs in order to prepare for a game or a season: a huge locker room, an equipment room, a training room where the head trainer and three assistants tape each player before practice and games, a weightlifting and exercise room, a coaches' locker room, an informal lounge with just enough comfort for card playing or reading, small meeting spaces, and a large lecture hall with tiered seats. In most of the rooms a coach is always within easy reach of a blackboard where he can diagram a play or maneuver.

The spacious building is where the players spend their football hours when they are not on the adjacent practice fields or actually in a game at the nearby stadium. If their injuries or bruises require it, they stop here in the morning between classes for special attention from the trainers. This is where they dress on Saturday mornings be-fore home games—and where they try to ease the tension by talking, joking, or playing cards.

The training quarters are usually full of noise—of clattering football shoes or hissing showers. On Sunday nights it is more quiet. The play-ers are anxious to see the films of themselves in yesterday's game and to see the reels showing their next opponent. It's a chance for them to judge their own work and that of the players they'll be facing in six days.

The lecture hall is divided into two sections of fifty-six seats. An accordion room divider can be pulled between the sections. There are separate projectors and screens on each side. The offensive players sit on one side, the defensive players on the other. When the films of the next opponent are shown, the defense watches only the offense; the offensive side studies the other team when it is playing defense. They will try to become familiar with the way their opponents look in various formations, their basic plays, and, finally, their individual habits. Sunday night is a get-acquainted meeting.

Coach Paterno stands at the side of one of the screens and looks up at the players. Except for a few shouts on the practice field during the week, it will be the last time he addresses the whole squad until the night before Saturday's game. He glances at his watch. It is a habit he will repeat dozens of times on the practice field during the week, as he rigidly follows the schedule he has mapped out.

"What time do we have?" he asks. "Seven-fourteen . . . Okay, let's go over some things." He quickly discusses a few changes in the starting time for practice, because of exams and an approaching holi-day. Then he turns to next Saturday's opponent. Penn State will be favored to win again, as the team has been throughout the season. He is certain of the players' confidence in their ability to win. He knows they have pride in their unbeaten record. He worries about a real letdown. He wants to make sure they respect their opponents.

"Now this is not the same team you saw last year," he begins. "They're better organized. They've stayed healthy. They don't do a lot of things, but they do them well. They're certainly not going to roll over and play dead on us. You're going to have to go in to them.

"Their tailback and quarterback—you'll have to gang-tackle them. Be around them and be sure! You'll have to rush their passer in the proper lane.

"This should be a good football game, the kind you enjoy. We'll work hard this week and when Saturday comes we'll go out and enjoy it. They'll play well for a while and then we'll see if they can keep it up when we put on the pressure. To do that we need a super week of practice."

He turns the meeting over to the two assistants and their movie projectors. The room divider is drawn between the aisles. The players hunch forward, elbows on the writing arms of their classroom seats. They'll see only part of yesterday's game before turning to the reels of their opponents in action in two or three recent games. They'll be encouraged to drop by the coaches' offices between classes during the week and study the films more carefully.

Coach Paterno leaves the sound of the two film projectors behind and heads for home. He has two reels with him he wants to see alone. Outside the wind has picked up and there are a few snowflakes in the November night air. Across the highway the steep sides of the stadium stand outlined by the glow of lights kept on above the press box. Will there be a rim of snow around the field at game time on Saturday?

2 | PRACTICE NO. 60

MONDAY'S WORKING hours begin well ahead of dawn for the coaches at Penn State. Joe Paterno is up at five-thirty, preparing the day's detailed practice schedule and shaping his thoughts for the morning-long meetings with his staff. If his two young sons in the family of five children don't interrupt too often, he can get a couple of hours of work done before the eight-o'clock meeting.

The assistant coaches go early to their offices in the Recreation Building, the old brick gymnasium known as Rec Hall, which stands atop the campus slope at State College, and sit down in front of the small film monitors on their desks. At this early stage of the game preparation, the coaches live inside 8-mm. film frames.

"Good morning, coaches' office," a secretary says over the phone minutes before eight o'clock. "No, he's going into a meeting. May I have him return your call?" The first phone call of the day and the competing sounds of the projectors in the back room signal the start of the work day.

The use of films in college football has increased the need for coaches to be ever more painstaking in the detailed preparation for a game. Few weaknesses or mistakes can be hidden from the movie camera. By careful study of game films, coaches can tell what teams do in most game situations—and exactly how they do it. A team's habits or "frequencies," the number of times a play or defense is used, are easily recorded. It is up to the coach to avoid letting his team's style of play fall into familiar patterns. His opponents are always "at the movies" too.

Before Paterno sits with the other coaches to talk about the week ahead, he takes care of a regular Monday publicity chore. In a back room of the Rec Hall he records comments on last Saturday's game and the next opponent. The recording is for the Penn State "Hot Line," a service for newspaper and radio and TV reporters. This time on the "Hot Line" he must also handle the question of another bowl bid for Penn State. Has Penn State already accepted an invitation to play on New Year's Day? Actually the players have met and voted their preference to go to the Orange Bowl. But bowl bids cannot officially be made or accepted for another several days, so Paterno must be diplomatic in his replies.

He is also careful in his comments to show respect for next Saturday's opponent. He knows they will be well prepared and anxious to upset Penn State. Paterno doesn't complain about playing the favorite's role, as some coaches do. He doesn't exaggerate his team's problems or injuries. Nor does he oversell the strength of his opponents. The press has come to expect him to speak as openly as he can about his team's chances. After finishing the recording he walks through the gym, where early-morning physical education classes are already under way. Some of the students in shorts and T shirts grin and wave a greeting. They're not the only ones whose work at the University starts early on Monday.

On the way to the meeting room Paterno pauses for a moment at an assistant's desk and watches the film monitor showing their opponents in a midseason game. He checks their formation, the Power I, and watches them move the ball well for several plays. "They certainly do like to run a lot," he comments.

The film monitors are turned off and the meeting starts a few minutes after eight. The coaches have filled their cups at the large coffee maker that was started early that morning. Paterno sits at the head of a table in front of the blackboard that stretches across the wall. Around him are the nine assistants who hold the special responsibilities for getting the team ready each week. Paterno has compared the job to that of rehearsing a symphony orchestra. "You work hard with the various parts during the week," he says, "and hope it all fits together on Saturday."

The assistants are in charge of offensive and defensive groups, made up of some eight to a dozen players each. They work with them on the practice field, hold short meetings before practice at the training quarters, review game films with them. Most of the coaches prepare instruction sheets for the players each week, diagramming the small changes in assignments for the game ahead. They worry about letdowns in individual performances during practice. They are concerned about injuries and morale, about special classroom or personal problems that affect their players. Some of the crises they will deal with themselves; others they will discuss with Paterno and let him handle.

Two of Paterno's assistants have been coaching at Penn State longer than he has. (He started as an assistant coach, teaching quarterbacks, in 1950.) All of them have worked together closely enough to know how much he expects in preparation for a game. John (J.T.) White, on the staff for more than twenty years, handles defensive ends. John Chuckran, a former Penn State halfback, coaches offensive guards and centers. Jerry Sandusky, another Penn State graduate, works with the linebackers. Bob Phillips, a former Pennsylvania high school coach, specializes in running backs and quarterbacks. Dick Anderson, a 1963 Penn State graduate, coaches offensive tackles and ends. Jim O'Hora, who has coached at Penn State since 1946, works with defensive linemen and calls the defenses from the sidelines during games. Frank Patrick, who played for Pittsburgh in the 1930s, coaches defensive backs. Booker Brooks, an offensive coach who specializes in wide receivers, takes to the road on weekends to scout Penn State's rivals. Fran Ganter's responsibilities are with the freshmen. A few of them get a chance to play with the varsity in their first year; all of them serve on the "foreign teams," the opponents' offense and defense, against the varsity during practice week.

Paterno's first concern this morning is with the freshmen. "I'll need a list of their exams," he tells Fran. The semester examinations in the next two weeks will prevent some of the freshmen from attending practice regularly. It is up to Fran to find enough time and enough players to prepare the foreign teams, so they can assume the opponents' defensive look and run their favorite plays. Serving on the foreign teams is an inglorious but necessary part of the training for freshmen.

The names and numbers of the opponents' offensive lineup are read; then the names of the Penn State freshmen who will play in their positions for the next few days. One of the freshmen will be moved up to the varsity because of an ankle injury to a starting defensive tackle. He will get special attention from Coach O'Hora all week long.

Paterno reads the practice schedule he filled in early in the morning at his home. It is a two-page guide for coaches and players that will account for every minute of practice time that afternoon, from 4:15 until 5:50. It is titled "Practice 60 (No Pads)"—the 60th practice of the season for Penn State; as usual, on Monday, the players will not be required to wear shoulder pads. While it is similar to other first-of-the-week schedules, the details show the areas Paterno feels need strengthening for Saturday's game. It also carries a small disciplinary note. In the top right-hand corner is a player's name and "Runs Laps (10)." The player, who was ten minutes late to Sunday's meeting, is being notified of the customary penalty—running a lap around the two practice fields for each minute of tardiness.

Paterno goes over the timetable for his assistants, commenting on the work he thinks needs particular attention. As soon as he finishes, a secretary will type and duplicate the schedule for coaches, managers, and players to refer to when they go to practice. To the stranger it reads like some highly technical work sheet to be understood only by advanced engineers.

"Okay, 4:15," Paterno begins. "Early group. Let's get the Xs, Ys, Zs catching." (X is the term for a flanker in the offensive lineup; Y is the tight end; Z the split end.) For just five minutes, from 4:15 until 4:20, they will practice their specialty—catching the ball and running with it. At 4:20 there will be ten minutes of pass-protection drills for offensive linemen. At the same time, on the defensive unit, the tackles and ends will go through their drills on rushing the passer. The linebackers will work on coverage of receivers.

"Let's start all over again," Paterno says to the defensive coaches. "We'll go back to the basics on defense." There is the edge of impatience in his voice, acquired after watching films and thinking about the defensive performance in Saturday's game. He mentions a linebacker. "Why, he acted as if he had never played the option before!"

Paterno says that individual drills, a regular segment of agility training at each practice, will run from 4:36 to 4:44. The printed schedule reveals how much each coach and each group of players is expected to accomplish in those eight minutes:

JOHN
Gs–Cs (*offensive guards, centers*)
Bull sled
Bag drill
Downfield Blocking
Blocks vs. Shields
(names of four reserve linebackers who will serve on defense with blocking shields)

DICK
Ts–Ys (*offensive tackles, tight ends*)
Bull sled
Boards
(names of reserves on defense)

BOOKER
Xs–Zs (*flankers, split ends*)
SC drill
Blocks vs. Shields
(names of four reserves on defense)

BOB
A–B–Qs (*tailbacks, fullbacks, quarterbacks*)
Ropes
Boards
Blocks vs. Shields
(names of three freshmen on defense)

F R A N
A–B
Quarterback option drill
(vs. three freshmen with shields)

J I M   O
Ts   (defensive tackles)
Takeoff
Seat rolls
Downfield Blocking
Follow leader
¼ Eagle

J T
Es–Rxs   (defensive ends, right tackles)
Quick Bags
Leverage
Key
Fall on Ball

J E R R Y   (with a graduate assistant)
B–F–M–H   (linebackers)
Mirror start
Score drill
Peel drill
Bounce

P A T   (with a graduate assistant)
L–S–R   (defensive halfbacks and safety)
1 on 2
Qb-End drill
Peel drill

After the individual drills—familiar agility tests which the coaches conduct at top speed—the "Teach" period runs from 4:44 to 4:56. This is a time the offense runs some of its basic plays against the opponents' normal defenses, and the defense gets a look at the opponents' offense as run by freshmen (foreign) teams. Paterno continues with the breakdown of the day's practice schedule—eight separate periods for the offense and defense during the hour and twenty minutes. The shortest drill is six minutes; the longest twenty.

"5:10 to 5:30," he says, "pass work. If it's a nice night, a little running." Which means the backs and ends will get a chance to let go against the simulated defense of the opponents.

The last drill for the offense, before the 5:50 end of practice, is two kickoff returns. The defense will practice covering two kickoffs: one a return along the sidelines, the other straight up the middle. The kickoff coverage had not been satisfactory on Saturday and the opponents were able to get good field positions against Penn State. Paterno lists the defensive players he wants in the kickoff-coverage practice. He stops at the name of one of the players who has a slight medical problem. "The doctor says it's a sugar deficiency. He can get weak and dizzy for short periods. I don't want him in there if he feels poorly."

He comes to another name on the coverage team. "Is he nervous because he's made mistakes?" he asks. "He goes all out to the 30 [yard line]. But the attack is to the 20! We just aren't adjusting to the long kickoffs." He turns to Booker Brooks and asks if the opponents have shown any reverses on their kickoff returns. The answer is no. Paterno wants the defense to get one onside kickoff. It will help keep them alert.

The next hours are devoted to the selection of defenses and offensive plays that will go into the game plan for Saturday. There will be changes—a play dropped or added, adjustments on defense—but the basic design will be set before the end of the day. It will determine the emphasis in practice through the week and with luck will work for Penn State on Saturday.

But before listing the defenses he wants in the game plan Paterno continues with his human concerns. What were the reasons for the weak performance last Saturday? "Are they playing tight?" he asks the four assistants seated with him. "Is it a question of confidence? We made mental mistakes. We weren't even lined up properly!"

He turns to individuals. "He never really hit anyone," he says. "Is it because he's that tense? He's had a couple of bad games, Jerry. Maybe you'd better give someone else a shot."

He asks about another player. "Does he have problems at home?" Jerry Sandusky will find out. If necessary, the player and Paterno will talk it over later on.

"Nobody's mean on the practice field. They've had it too easy," he continues. "All that stuff about being No. 1!" His voice trails off. The room is quiet for a moment, except for the clacking sound of the duplicating machine, turning out the day's schedule. Penn State's defense has a reputation as the best in college football. The coaches around the table have brought it to that excellence. On this Monday morning they are being reminded that the defense was not good enough.

Paterno turns to the blackboard. He lists the defenses, 1 through 13, he wants to play on Saturday. This late in the season the technical names have become as familiar to the players as those of close campus friends: 8 Rotate, 6T Rotate, 6 Blow, State Super, 50 Web, State Bullet, etc. But each defense demands a lot from the eleven players on the field—precise lining up, a series of quick mental and physical reactions, complete follow-through. Because of exams during the week, Paterno wants to keep the list of defenses short for Saturday. He wants to go with the familiar and not add anything. Yet there must be defenses enough to handle the opponents' running and passing game.

"How good a runner is the quarterback?" he asks. The opinion is that he runs well enough but hasn't had much help from the offensive line. "Their backs make some good cuts," Paterno adds, recalling an impression formed while watching films at home. "And that tailback—he ran all over us two years ago!"

He throws out more questions at the staff: How much wingback do they use? Do they hook the end? How good a blocker is their tight end? Is he good on sweeps, on straight hits? Then he asks if the breakdowns are ready on the last game they played—how much did they gain against what type of defense?

The breakdowns for the last meeting between Penn State and the rivals are available. "We used the 6 Stitch thirty times against them two years ago," Fran Ganter reports. "They gained 170 yards on the ground. We had six intercepts on them. They threw a lot to the sidelines. They had a 47-yard run against us. We were in the 6 Stitch. They were unbalanced. I'm sure we'll see more of that on Saturday."

Paterno reviews the thirteen defenses on the board with J. T. White, Jerry Sandusky, Jim O'Hora, and Frank Patrick. They stare at the board in silence for a while. "Let's go with what they know," Paterno says. "Let's try not to add this week."

It is time, at 10:10, for him to spend an hour or more with the offensive coaches. Before he makes the switch from defense to offense the entire staff observes a Monday ritual. When Penn State wins on Saturday one of the secretaries bakes a cake over the weekend and everyone in the office is invited to have a piece. There hasn't been a Monday morning without cake all season long.

In the room where the offensive coaches have been arranging the plays they think should be used on Saturday, the lists fill most of two blackboards. There are seventeen running plays on one board, thirteen passes on another. There are "short yardage" plays and plays to be used when Penn State is within five yards of the goal line. Paterno asks about the condition of his tailback, the hardest and busiest runner on the team. "I didn't get a chance to talk to him at the meeting last night," he says. "Did he come out all right?" The tailback has some bruises but he is generally okay. (After the game on Saturday the trainer had applied four cold packs to reduce the swelling on various parts of his arms, shoulders, and legs.)

This morning's business for the offense is filled with the tiny adjustments needed to make Penn State's basic plays work best against the opponents' defenses. There are problems because of the way they "stack" their men on defense, making it harder for a Penn State lineman to see how he should follow through on his blocking assignment. "On 31G, can we get a Dave call?" someone at the table asks. A "Dave" call is one of the code signals which lets the linemen know how they can help one another after they have taken their position. A "Dave" call from the tackle on 31G, which the quarterback has given in the huddle, tells the tight end he should vary his blocking slightly because of the way the linebackers are positioned. A "George" call from guard to center may inform the center that because of a shift by the defense he will be blocking without help on a play.

The play, 31G, is diagrammed on the board against other defenses the opponents are likely to use. It is tested against minor variations— with the "nose" man (the defensive middle guard) playing squarely across the line from Penn State's center and with the "nose" man slightly away.

"Bob, can we tell the quarterback to call an automatic when he sees the "nose" playing here?" Paterno asks coach Bob Phillips. An automatic, a switch from one play to another at the line of scrimmage, will take advantage of the slight move by the "nose" man. That afternoon at three Phillips will go over the opponents' films with his quarterbacks and discuss the need for an automatic in this situation, one of the changes they must keep in mind for Saturday.

"Is there anyone weak in that secondary?" Paterno asks. "Anyone we should pick on?" The opponents do have several young players on defense who do not react as well as others. The weaker areas will be given particular attention on run and pass plays.

It is nearing noon when Paterno returns to the meeting of the defensive coaches, in time to hear statistics based on the films which help explain what the opponents like to do when they have the ball. In a recent game they had fifty-one runs and only seven passes when they were in the Power I formation. In the slot formation they passed more often. Their quarterback likes to let his tailback carry the ball or run with it himself. He seldom drops straight back and passes. How much poise does he seem to have? Can Penn State afford to "go after him"— and risk leaving gaps in their pass coverage?

The talk is interrupted by the appearance of Chuck Medlar, the team's head trainer, who coaches Penn State baseball in the spring. Medlar has a Monday report on the condition of the players, with a few added casualties. A wide receiver has a bad foot. "Something snapped when he pushed off. He's hurting. We'll know more on Wednesday." An offensive lineman may have to stay on crutches through most of the week with an ankle injury. "That leg of his has gone through hell," Paterno says. An offensive center has a cut hand and should take a day off from snapping the ball. The quarterback and the running backs are in great shape.

"Don't talk about it," one of the coaches says, knocking on the wooden table.

It's 12:30 and Paterno has been playing next Saturday's game in his mind for nearly seven hours. But there are a few more questions before the lunch break. Have they seen anything in the way the opponents kick extra points which they could take advantage of? Could they block the kick?

"The right guard does lean toward center," Jim O'Hora says. "Once they did fake the placement and throw a pass," he adds. That small threat will be passed on to the defensive secondary.

THE BLUE-AND-WHITE sign on the fence reads: "Varsity Football Practice Field—Others Stay Off." Actually there are three fields behind the steel fence adjacent to the training quarters. One is of artificial turf and is used when Penn State is preparing for an away game to be played on similar ground cover, or when the two fields of natural grass are in poor shape because of severe weather conditions. The field of artificial turf is also used by other athletic teams at the University, such as the soccer squad.

Although the area is tucked off in a corner of the campus, away from most student traffic, it does not have the closed, walled appearance of many big university practice fields. It has few of the modern mechanical devices favored by some teams. There is no coach's tower where the head coach stands and directs practice like a remote movie director, shouting instructions through a bull horn at the players below. At Penn State coaches, players, and managers work together on fields rimmed with light poles. And in November the lights go on early at practice.

At three in the afternoon the fields are empty, except for the scattered blocking sleds, bags, running ropes, tackle stick that will be used later on. One figure jogs hurriedly around the perimeter of the fields. He is defensive coach Jerry Sandusky, "getting rid of a little tension" before practice week begins. After his run Sandusky will go into the training quarters for the first of a series of pre-practice meetings with his linebackers. He will introduce them to the changes in assignment and special problems they will face during the week—and at game time on Saturday. The other assistants will use fifteen or twenty minutes of the time until 4:15 for similar talks or a look at films with their players.

The one hour and thirty-five minutes of practice on Monday seems as intense as a regular game. Everything is run at full speed. It is Paterno's way of making the players do in practice exactly as they would do in a game. "Practice good to play good" is a saying a player learns early at Penn State. He also learns there is no room in practice for mental errors. He gets "up" for a game by staying "up" in practice all week long. Practice does not mean running a play over and over again until it is perfect. At this stage of the season the coaches are looking for perfection in every play.

Practice begins with the "every day" drills: ends and backs catching lob passes with one hand, quarterbacks taking the snap from centers, defensive backs "intercepting" passes thrown by coaches or graduate assistants. Like so many circus performers working on their special acts, the players give style and grace to these drills.

At exactly 4:30 the entire squad goes into its stretch drill, led by Coach Sandusky. This is a peppery six-minute period of muscle toning and stretching. It is moderate exercise compared with the heavy calisthenics which the team goes through in preseason. It is a time of togetherness, with the coaches participating, joining in the chatter and cadenced hand clapping.

At Monday morning meeting, Coach Paterno outlines the day's practice schedule with his assistants

Coach Paterno worries about defensive mistakes that must be corrected before Saturday's game

At the first meeting each morning, all coaches on offense and defense meet and exchange ideas

Coach Paterno spends at least one busy hour each day an-swering phone calls and seeing visitors in his office

*In the coaches' locker room, Coach Paterno and an assistant
meet before taking the field for practice*

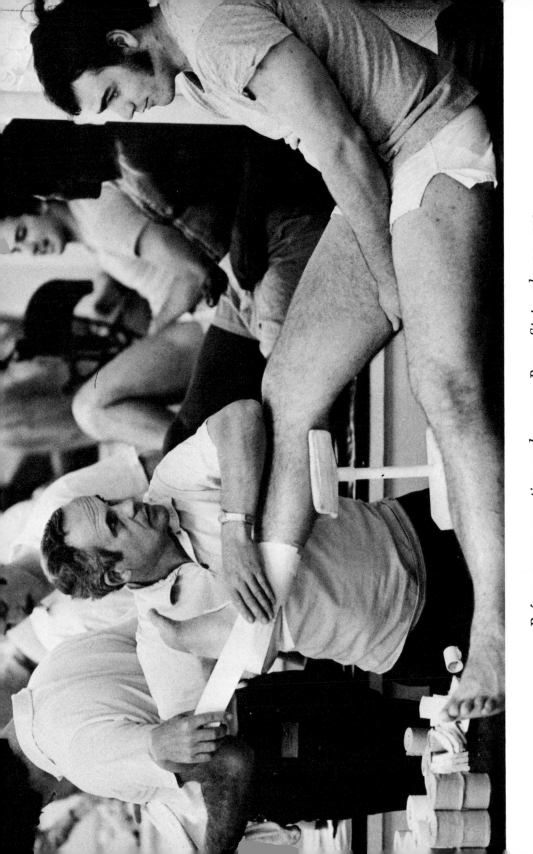

Before every practice and game, Penn State players are quickly, expertly taped

A bruised shoulder gets special attention from the team's head trainer, Chuck Medlar

The practice pace picks up sharply in the agility drills that run from 4:36 to 4:44. The nine assistants work separately with their groups. Paterno moves from one to another, prodding or encouraging. "Zip!" he yells. "Let's have more zip." At 4:44 by his watch, he signals for a change and the small units quickly fit into teams for the Teach period. The first-string offensive team huddles in light-blue jerseys; the others in light green. The defensive teams, on a separate field, are in dark blue and dark red. The freshmen on the foreign teams wear white with black numbers the same as those used by the opponents.

At 5:10 another hand clap and yell of "Let's go!" from Paterno shifts the emphasis to drills against the visitors' offense and defense. Penn State's first line and backs work their pass plays against the foreign team. The defense—one team in red, the other in blue—protect their goal line against the opponents' favorite touchdown plays. To help the freshmen on the offensive foreign team get quickly acquainted with the plays, assistants show them diagrams in the huddle.

It all seems to run like high-speed clockwork. But the shouts of the coaches tell of frustration and error.

"Don't be sloppy. Fake that draw!"

"Get to the ball. Be there! Be there!"

No shrill whistles are blown; no shouts of profanity come from coaches. But the messages are clear.

At the side of the field the lineman whose ankle strain keeps him on crutches follows the work of the first-team offensive line. A senior who has earned a starting position at guard, he is very anxious to be able to play in the last game or two of the season. He's not sure how fast the ankle will heal, but he stays mentally prepared by attending meetings with the guards and centers and by watching at practice.

The look of the opponents' defense is familiar to him. It is the Oklahoma or Gap 7 defense and he has faced it many times. But he needs to be sure of the characteristics of the players he will face. After daily pre-practice meetings with coach Dick Anderson at the blackboard, the Xs and Os, showing how they line up, will be set in his mind. The study of films again later in the week will give him a clearer picture of his opponent. Maybe when he faces him across the scrimmage line on Saturday he'll be able to tell just by the way his opponent places his hand whether he'll rush inside or outside.

In his first year on the team he used to wonder why he had to go over the same moves again and again. For an offensive lineman the moves on different plays seemed to change little. Paterno prodded him, "Be better. Be better!" It wasn't until he became much better at technique that he knew what the coach had meant.

THE LAST work of the day, a kickoff return, sends the ball spiraling high into the lights that surround the field. Paterno watches the deep kick and the ball carrier run swiftly up the sideline behind a fence of blockers. It looks good.

"Go ahead in, fellows!" he yells. "See you tomorrow." The players head for the gate leading to the training quarters. The manager and five or six assistants begin to pick up balls and equipment. Around the darkening edge of the field the tardy defensive halfback begins running the first of his ten laps.

"You don't have to do them all tonight," Paterno tells him.

3 | BLOODY TUESDAY

T HE PLAYERS call it Bloody Tuesday. "If you get by Tuesday and then Wednesday," they say, "there's relief the rest of the week." Tuesday holds the longest, hardest practice, a day of cracking down by the coaches. The game plan is set. The coaches are anxious to set the tone on the practice field for the game on Saturday.

This Tuesday will be more uncomfortable than most for both players and coaches. At the morning meeting Paterno announces he wants to meet with the defense at 3:50 that afternoon, fifteen minutes before the start of practice. It's time, he's decided, to talk to them about their attitude and last Saturday's game. Paterno seldom gives "pep talks" to the squad. But he is, according to those who play for him, "a master at the mental side of the game. He knows precisely when you need to be told you're doing well. He knows when it's time to criticize."

His review of the practice schedule this morning brings out sharp complaints:

"We need more work on extra points. Is he kicking through the ball or punching it? There's *something* wrong. He can't seem to guide it. The ball is set okay.

"Take the ends and work on options. We've got to do better." He taps the table with his fist and says, "The more I watched the films last night, the madder I got."

The opponents' option plays, in which the quarterback runs laterally behind the line and either keeps the ball himself or pitches it out to one of his backs, hurt Penn State. If ends or linebackers react too soon, the option play can break a defense wide open.

"The end and outside linebacker must close that cavity," he says. "The E Go wasn't working either." (E Go is releasing the end and letting him force the quarterback to make the option.) "It wasn't his fault. I'm not blaming him. It was our fault it didn't work.

"I want everyone to get the fall-on-the-ball drill today. And let's get some good goal-line tackling.

"Make that foreign team go all out. We're going to hit them this week."

One of the graduate assistants reports that a freshman on the defensive team was pulling his shield during Monday's practice. The shield is used to reduce the chance of injury when blocks are thrown. Monday's practice was without shoulder pads, making the blocking shields more important as protection. Paterno says he wants to talk with the player. "If you find anybody who's not all business, let's make a switch right there on the field. If we're going to get beat we get beat with the people who came to play."

The meeting breaks up. The offensive coaches take their pads and coffeecups and go into a separate room. Paterno stays with the defense. The talk for the next hour or more will center on the responsibilities of the end and linebacker vs. the option. It's time to argue all over again the way these positions are to be played in the thirteen defenses Penn

State now expects to use on Saturday. The give-and-take among the coaches will bring changes that involve inches in the way the players line up.

"There's too much area between the guy who's making the quarterback pitch and the man who's playing the pitch," Paterno says.

"The end can't be a superman," J. T. White says. "He needs help from the backer and tackle."

"Should we widen a little with the end?" Paterno goes to the board and diagrams the defense with the end slightly to the outside. He studies it for a moment. "I'll give you that." The tiny changes in alignment will be given to the ends before practice that afternoon and noted in their game instruction sheets later.

"Here's another problem," Sandusky says. "If they run the down-the-line option, the Hero gets turned. . . ."

"The end didn't help him."

"The Hero has to squeeze it. He has to make the play," Paterno says.

In the Penn State defense the four linebackers bear different names, indicating where they line up. The Hero is the outside linebacker who faces the heavy side of the offensive formation, with the flanker and split end. Fritz is the name of the outside linebacker on the other side, facing the offensive tight end. Mike is the linebacker next to the Hero. The other inside linebacker is called simply the Backer. He is sometimes a rover.

Coach Jim O'Hora wonders whether the defensive game plan needs both the 6 Gun and the 6 Blow. It opens up a twenty-minute discussion on how much will be lost if one of the defenses is dropped. The coaches study the list of defenses, the scribbles on the board that show the option play against the end and the Hero. Finally Paterno agrees. The 6 Gun is erased from the list.

Paterno turns to the offense at the other end of the coaches' office.

Booker Brooks, who has been looking at films for a scouting report on Penn State's opponent two weeks ahead, also joins the meeting.

"Have you guys scored any points yet?" Paterno greets the offensive coaches. He glances at the board, where one more running play has been added to the original list of seventeen. The coaches have selected five "goal line" plays, including one when Penn State has a third down and five yards to go for a touchdown and another when it is third down and eight yards to go.

Paterno is anxious to know who in the opponents' defense can be picked on. "Would you run here or here?" he asks, indicating the linebackers in their Oklahoma defense.

"The right side has no feet," one of the coaches comments. "In the clutch we should go right."

"26 gets beat a lot," Booker says.

"So we get 26 where?" Paterno asks, wondering what passes will work against the defensive back. They discuss adding a fake to one of their regular pass plays to take advantage of the slow reaction of No. 26. Paterno agrees but says, "If we can put it in quickly, fine. If we need to throw ten passes in practice to get it right, forget it. We don't have the time."

Before the meeting ends at about noon, Paterno and Bob Phillips talk about their tailback, who carried the ball nearly forty times on Saturday. "He looked tired last night," Bob says. "But he claims he wasn't tired after the game. He didn't realize he had carried the ball that much. You know what he was really proud of? The two blocks he put on their tackle!"

Paterno and Phillips take pride in the tailback, who has handled the heavy load on offense all season and has stood up so well under the pressure. He has been burdened with too much attention from both the public and Penn State's opponents.

"Looking at him on films last night," Paterno says, "I realized that little stutter step of his was getting seven yards when he should have had only two."

There are always calls and usually visitors waiting when Paterno leaves the morning meetings and returns to his own office.

A man in work clothes greets him and says the last time they met was at the state prison. Paterno had been there to talk to the inmates. The former prisoner was proud to say he was out and had a job at the University. "Would you have three tickets to the game on Saturday?" he asks.

Paterno smiles at the familiar question. "I really don't know what we have now," he replies. "Call the office on Thursday."

A slender student, books under his arm, wants to know if there's a chance to start a "lightweight" football program at the University. "They told me I was too small to try out for the regular team," he says.

"Why don't you work with the weights this winter," Paterno says. "Then come out for the team in the spring." The student says he'd like to try.

Before Paterno goes home for his usual lunch of yogurt, the assistant athletic director comes in to discuss a Pennsylvania high school prospect. Should he talk to the boy and encourage him about entering Penn State next fall?

"Sure," Paterno says, "but encourage him to get his grades up if he wants to play here."

A

SSISTANT COACH Frank Patrick hunches over the projector at the training quarters, preparing the opponents' film for the defensive backs at the 2:45 meeting he has called. He has copies of the completed defensive game plan, two pages of single-spaced instruction. It is crammed with the science of football and with terms that are familiar only to the players and coaches at Penn State.

For the defensive backs many of the details of the game plan began to take shape at Monday's practice. The copy of the plan which they will study at their lockers or in their dorms, the films they watch during the week, and the continual talks with Coach Patrick all help to set their jobs firmly in mind. At practice and at Saturday's game it's a matter of concentration.

The game plan covers changes in the team's normal lineup rules. It lists the defenses to be used on "color calls." A color call—Blue, Gray, Black—from the defensive captain can suddenly change the defense they are in. For example, if the opponents line up quickly without a huddle, a yell of "Blue" changes the rushing (or blitzing) defense to a cautious "prevent" defense. The prevent is designed to stop the desperation pass or trick play from scoring a touchdown. The game plan includes the small changes the coaches have decided upon for each of the twelve defenses Penn State may use on Saturday.

Here is the game plan instruction the defensive team must keep in mind in its pass coverage against the opponents' "fly" (pass receiver lines up unusually wide):

> If Penn State is in a 6 Tough, 6 Gap, 6 Blow defense, it
> shifts to ½ coverage on the side of the fly. If the defense
> called is 50 Web or 50 Fritz or 50 Rotate and the fly

lines up to the Hero's side, the coverage originally called
stays. If the fly lines up away from the Hero, the defense
goes to "web" coverage. If the defense is a 3-deep prevent coverage against the pass, it stays the same.

There are more than forty separate instructions, such as the one
above, in the game plan. They cover everything from goal-line defenses to punt-blocking attempts. Also included is the weekly reminder to the defense that if they see the opponents go into an unusual
lineup ("garbage" is the term for crazy formations), they are to go
automatically to a prevent defense.

Coach Patrick reviews the game plan with his defensive halfbacks
and safety men seated in front of the screen. They are half dressed for
practice, wearing T shirts and football pants. For a few minutes they
will mentally play defense against the opponents by watching their
offense on film. Patrick keeps a running barrage of questions and comment going as the film unwinds:

"All right, we have a State Blitz. What's your call, Tom?" he asks a
safety man. "Bill's going to do what to that outside man?

"We're in 8 Rotate. Give me your call, Jack. Now off that play
action they have a little pop pass. So watch it!

"If their man [the split end] is three yards from the sideline, you
play him where? Right, on the inside.

"They've got fast backs. Don't underestimate that speed.

"They're slot right. If we're in a 50 Web it goes to what? 50 Rotate.
That's right.

"Be sure you communicate with the Fritz.

"Here's their quarterback keeper. Don't go to sleep! Don't put your
nose in there. See what happens!" (On the screen the quarterback
keeps the ball and goes outside for a long gain because a defensive

back "put his nose in there" and tried to make a tackle instead of holding his ground.)

"If their man [the split end] is three yards from the sideline, you play him where? Yes, on the inside."

The coach and his defensive backs play the game together for three reels. Later in the afternoon many of the plays they saw on the screen will come at them "live" as the foreign team runs through the opponents' offense.

SINCE SUNDAY, Paterno has been waiting for this hour to talk to the defense. The veterans on the team sensed it was coming before the meeting was announced. They have been through it before on a few occasions. They may think they've been driving just as hard as the offensive team toward excellence. But something has gone wrong. It showed last Saturday when their opponents kept the pressure on the defense throughout the game. The meeting can be an uncomfortable time but they will be the better for it on the field later. Paterno never gives them a tough talking to unless he feels they need it.

At 3:30 the defensive players in their dark-colored practice jerseys trail out of the locker room and take the steps up to their seats in the lecture hall. In their broad shoulder pads and white pants they make the seats seem as small as kindergarten chairs. They wear the solemn faces of small boys about to be sharply disciplined by their teacher.

Paterno asks one of the assistants to close the door. He begins bluntly. "I've told the coaches that if they see anyone not giving a hundred percent this week they should drop him. Put someone else in right away. We'll go with those who want to play. There's been too much coaching by you fellows out there. I hear it all the time—'You take the pitch. You do this. . . .' You happen to have the best defensive coaches in the country. Listen to them from now on.

"In practice, we're not hitting. We're going through the motions. And it shows on Saturday. The second, the third man through isn't popping. That's why we're not getting turnovers. You're not hitting hard enough. I haven't seen any gang tackling. No one's punishing anybody." The familiar voice is loud, controlled.

Paterno teams at Penn State have taken much pride in their ability to take the play away from opponents late in the game. Many of the victories have come after the team has trailed by a touchdown or more at halftime. The whole preparation program, from spring practice through the last week's work in November, is geared to Penn State's being physically stronger and mentally sharper than its opponents during the last twenty or thirty minutes of football. When Penn State turns on the pressure in the second half, most teams have not been able to stay with them.

"Some of you, after the game two weeks ago, were saying, 'They ran out of tricks and had to come at us.' Well, they came at you Saturday all afternoon long," he continues. "We could have been using twelve men on the field and they still would have been coming. They weren't about to quit. I can't remember a game in recent years when I felt we weren't stronger at the end.

"Some of you believed you were going to be the best defensive team in football. You began reading you were the best and subconsciously you began believing you were. But like everything else in life, the payoff is only on performance. . . .

"I know you've all worked hard to be here, to come this far toward excellence. It's up to you to prove to yourselves it's been worth it."

It is four o'clock and time for work. Paterno is silent for a moment. "All right," he says more quietly, "let's have a good practice." As the defensive players return to their lockers to pick up their helmets, one of them glances at the schedule for Practice No. 61. In the corner of the sheet is the note: "Must have good option period." Paterno has listed himself as one of the coaches who will work with ends and Fritz linebackers in the option drills.

Tuesday practice, like the others during the week, builds in momentum from the early pass-catching and fall-on-ball drills to the twenty or thirty minutes of "Thud" at the end. The Thud is what it sounds like—running the offense and defense "live" against the foreign teams. It is the closest Penn State comes to the old-fashioned practice scrimmage during the season.

This Tuesday practice has a brisker tempo than usual. On the field where the defense works, the sounds of contact sharpen as the Mikes, Heroes, Fritzes, ends, tackles slam into the shields handled by the freshmen. The defense, coaches, members of the foreign team, even the managers who hustle in and out making sure there is always an available football, sense the combative mood. When Paterno claps his hands and yells for the start of the Teach period at 4:34, one of the assistants says:

"Wow, the whiteys are all juiced up, too!" The freshmen don't intend to let the varsity defense go at them without giving a lot in return.

The Thud, the last period of practice, from 5:20 to 5:50 for the offense and 5:39 to 5:50 for the defense, seems as intense as a Saturday game. As Penn State's offense runs six goal-line plays, the white-shirted freshmen on defense try to grab the ball, forcing fumbles.

Meanwhile, the defense slams into the foreign team as it runs a sequence of ten plays favored by the opposition.

At 5:50 Paterno calls a halt. "Okay, hit the stick and in, fellows. A good job. Good job!"

Hitting the stick is an end-of-practice ritual on Tuesday and Wednesday. The tackle stick waits near the gate to the field and each player is required to slam into it twice before going to the locker room. In the darkness of this evening the tackling stick takes an especially hard pounding.

Paterno follows the team, keyed up and noisy, into the warmth of the locker room. He has gotten immediate results from the defense. They worked and concentrated hard; the foreign team gave them stiff competition. Now he wonders how he can keep the offensive players from suffering a letdown. As a long season comes to an end it isn't easy for coaches and players to hold on to their resolve. The difference between going through the motions, which they now know well, and really applying muscle and spirit to the job can be a thin line. Often enough the coaches can't tell which way it will be until Saturday after one o'clock.

A T H I S locker, the first-team tailback slowly removes his pads and pants for the welcome shower. His legs feel heavy, as they had throughout practice. His mind wasn't sharp either. He ruined a good block to the outside by his right tackle when he failed to cut in quickly enough. He was trying to run the play to perfection, just as he would in a game, but his legs and mind wouldn't let him.

He has felt this physical and mental letdown before at midweek. On Sunday he was concerned about the turnovers the offense made in the game and their failure to move the ball in the last quarter. Usually when Penn State wins he can leave the game on the field. But the interviews with the press and the growing weariness made it impossible for him to put it out of his mind. Wednesday and Thursday will be different, he hopes. He has learned after playing for Paterno for three years that the only way he can get "up" for a game is to be good in practice. He wants to get that edge, so that on Friday, the welcome day off, he will know he is ready again.

4 | A TEST FOR A
HERO

"THIS IS a funny film," the sophomore linebacker exclaims. "I'm so busy watching the other team's blitzing linebacker jump off-side, I'm not watching the pass plays. Look, there he goes! Offside again!"

It is before the coaches' morning meeting, set for 8:30 on Wednesday, and the linebacker has come to Frank Patrick's desk projector to study the opponents' pass patterns. He always studies two or three reels of film on his own during the middle of the week. This morning he stopped in early before going to the library to prepare for an exam. He is, for the moment, distracted by watching someone else play the same position he does. One of the coaches says he won't see a lot of pass offense on the films. "But watch the way they run the option."

The coaches leave the linebacker at the projector and file into the meeting room. The linebacker is one of several players who will drop by for a study of the opponents on film during the morning.

Paterno takes out the practice schedule he drew up at home. He says he will take an early group at 4:15—the Fritz linebackers and ends—and drill on the options. Then he, J. T. White, and Jerry Sandusky will work with groups against a mix of options and pass plays. "Later," he says to the defensive coaches, "I want to argue with you about the width of the Hero. Where we have him lined up now."

The heavy schedule includes one look for the players at a number of surprise situations which often develop in a game: a kick and a return following a safety, a ten-man rush of the punter in an attempt to block a kick, a fake kick and run, a kick from deep in the end zone, among others. If rehearsed once on Wednesday, they will be handled more efficiently on Saturday.

Before the offensive coaches go on to their own meeting, Paterno wants to know if they were, perhaps, throwing too many deep passes and not enough "curls" in practice. "I know we had one last night that was badly timed," he adds. One badly timed pass in practice is one too many.

Paterno turns to the game of inches and yards on defense.

"I watched that Hero yesterday," he begins. "We don't have him lined up right." He compares two of the defenses in the game plan for Saturday and then goes to the board and draws the problem in Os, Es, and Hs:

$$
\begin{array}{ccc}
\text{SE} & & 0 \quad 0 \quad 0 \quad 0 \\
\downarrow & & \text{E} \\
& \leftarrow \text{Hero} &
\end{array}
$$

"We'd expect him to cover that, wouldn't we?" (Hero to cover the split end), he says. "Why don't we have him line up five yards outside the end? Let the Hero take chances to the inside and make the play go outside. Now on 50 Rotate we have another ball game. He has to make that play go inside. Don't change the 50 Rotate lineup."

Paterno, Jerry Sandusky, and Jim O'Hora begin to worry about the body angle of the Hero as he lines up in the various defenses. And maybe they should change the stance of the end slightly and get him down lower? The end and the tackle—can't they close it up so that they're only two feet apart?

The coaches review the way they want the Hero to line up in the defenses that will be most used on Saturday. The changes will give Penn State a slightly different look on defense, which will become noticeable to the opponents during the game and will be picked up on film by future opponents. They are part of the constant changes that are made to meet problems, such as the weakness Penn State showed against the option play.

These are some of the lineup responsibilities the players at the Hero position will keep in mind on Saturday:

> If the defense is 8 Rotate—Hero lines up on the strong
> side
> 6 Tough Rotate—line up away from tight end
> and outside eye of tight end
> Gap Tough Rotate—away from tight end, outside
> half of end who is tight
> 50 Rotate—strong side
> 50 Web—line up a little wider
> 50 Fritz Blow—wider
> State Super—line up in State position
> away from tight end

> State Blitz—line up away from tight end
> and inside the slot
> Prevent—line up on widest receiver
> to the strong side

The Hero must make other adjustments, from one to five yards, if he is faced with "twins" in the opponents' formation. Twins are two receivers, an end and a flanker, who take positions wide to the same side.

After he is lined up, the Hero must assume the proper body angle and remember his "key" for the particular defense he is in. The key is what he reacts to when the offense begins its play. It may be the move by the tailback or the tight end or the snap of the ball, which he keeps his eyes on by looking through the legs of a defensive tackle on the line of scrimmage.

His job then depends on the play that develops—a straight run, a sweep, an option, a pass. For example, his instructions when he faces the option play in one defense are: "Come straight up square. Not too deep. Play lead block with hands. Give off, staying square. Make the pitch go deep and to the outside, if anywhere."

The instruction to the Backer in another defense: "Against the run— if action is to you, slide to nose of tackle. Stay square. Pursue from inside out. If action is away from you, scrape nose of center, get squared up when blocked."

Jerry Sandusky will go over the agreed-upon changes of assignment with the linebackers before practice. The changes will go into the instruction sheet he prepares each week for the Backers, Fritzes, Mikes, Heroes. It is their own detailed position guide to the game on Saturday, which they can study at their lockers or while they are being taped for practice.

Paterno now makes the Wednesday-morning review of the defense game plan which Frank Patrick assembled.

"They did well last night," Paterno says to his four assistants at the table. "Let's keep after them."

The review of the written game plan includes running comment and questions among the coaches.

"How big is that tailback?"

"He's six feet, 195."

"The quarterback runs better than he passes, doesn't he? They like their sweeps and pitches."

"Is there any pattern at the goal line when they run outside so we can go into an 8 Rotate?"

"The wingback doesn't block the corner—he hooks."

"What else do you think we might use on the eight- or nine-yard line?"

"The 50 scares me against the power sweep."

"Surely we can beat them, man for man, when you look at their blocking."

"Let's always assume they're better than we think they are."

The conversation turns to a player problem on the defensive team. One of the ends, young and talented, has been showing little discipline in practice. "He was taking a jump at the quarterback last night," one of the coaches says. "He knows he should stay put."

"One trouble is he's so quick—and he knows it. He can run right around a block."

"He'll argue with you that it can be done his way."

"Let's talk to him, not argue with him."

Coach Paterno has two more player problems waiting for him in his office after the meeting. One is a request to be excused from practice. The player says he would like to attend the funeral of a high school friend who was killed in a car accident. Paterno wants to find out how important it is to the player that he attend the funeral before he decides. He wants to make sure it isn't just an excuse to get out of practice.

Missing practice because of an exam, unusual class conflict, injury, or illness is common enough. Other reasons for being absent need to be fully explained to Paterno before he approves. Earlier in the season he excused his No. 1 place kicker from an away game because the player said he preferred to be with the soccer team on that Saturday. The kicker is also an All-American soccer player. Paterno felt he should have the right to choose which sport he wanted to play at Penn State.

A freshman player drops by to say that "everything is going okay." He has his courses straightened out and a make-up exam scheduled.

"You look fine," Paterno says. "I'm glad it's working out."

Behind the greeting is a problem that Paterno faces every so often with his young players at Penn State. It is a problem that comes with continued success in football.

As an excellent high school player the year before, the freshman was one of the most sought-after backs in the state. Paterno visited his home town and talked to him about coming to Penn State. The player said he had many scholarship offers. Besides, he was worried that he might have to cut his hair too short if he decided to go to Penn State. Paterno said there were team requirements on hair length but that he would have to cut it very little. He showed him how little.

The star halfback finally decided to go to Penn State and he accepted one of the twenty-six scholarships for in-coming freshmen. But not many weeks after he joined the large, white-shirted freshman squad he began to develop problems. He complained of a pulled muscle, then other minor ailments. In practice he showed less and less of the talent that had made him such an outstanding high school player.

A few days ago, Paterno got a call from the boy's high school coach. The player had left Penn State and gone home. He said he was too discouraged by his injuries to continue. Paterno immediately contacted the freshman and discussed his injuries and his standing on the freshman team. He could see that the real problem was the player's lack of confidence. When someone else was moved ahead of him to the varsity he got discouraged and quit. He used the injuries as an excuse to explain to friends why he had come home.

Paterno told the freshman that his situation was not unique. "It happens to many good players who come here. They see others who are just as good on the field. They get discouraged because they're not playing all the time, as they did in high school. If everyone who became discouraged, who got down on himself, dropped off the squad, we wouldn't have many players left. At one point or another it happens to almost every member of the team."

For Paterno the crisis in the life of the freshman player was a familiar case of morale. He and the other coaches work hard to keep morale at a high level throughout the squad. "You don't have to concern yourself much with how a first-stringer feels," he says. "The real test is whether the last substitute has good morale. If he has, it means everybody has."

After his talk with the discouraged freshman, Paterno had conversations with the high school coach, the principal, and the boy's father. They all agreed he should re-enter the university immediately, even though he had missed important classes at the end of the term. Paterno called the dean at the university to make sure the boy wouldn't be heavily penalized just because he was a football player.

It was agreed he could make up courses and take a make-up exam, which would cost him a small fee. He could concentrate on his class work and report to the team at spring practice.

EACH WEDNESDAY noon Coach Paterno, one of his assistants, and one of his players attend the Quarterback Club luncheon at the Inn on the edge of the campus. The public appearance is part of the coach's job of keeping university people and residents of the town involved with the football program at Penn State. Later in the day he will talk to a much wider audience on a weekly TV program.

At the luncheon the informal comment by coaches and player and the questions from club members are about the game of last Saturday. First the player Paterno has brought along as a guest, the team's fast punt-return specialist, talks about his job. "It's mostly a matter of never getting into any bad habits," he says, "like not concentrating. If you concentrate you're not apt to drop the football. That goes for pass catching too."

"Do you prefer to run to the right or the left when you return punts?" a luncheon member asks.

"Neither one," the player says with a wide grin. "Straight up the middle is what I prefer."

Coach Dick Anderson discusses briefly his work with the offensive tackles and ends, who, along with the guards and the center, have the less glamorous jobs on the team. A team's offense is only as good as its offensive line. Anderson says that at Penn State they try to break the job down into simple parts, so there are a minimum of adjustments. The perfection of blocking technique continues all season long; the preparation for each opponent changes from week to week. He says that he and Coach John Chuckran have spent a lot of time in the last three days watching the visitors on film to see why they do so much "stunting" on defense. Are their stunts an attempt to cover up weaknesses or lack of experience in some areas?

Coach Paterno tells the audience that Penn State faced a very good offensive line last Saturday. Yes, the defense had trouble handling the Veer-type attack. A simple but serious problem had come up during the game, one the coaches and players were working to correct: On the option play there was too much area between the player who was forcing the quarterback to make the pitch to his back and the linebacker who was then responsible for playing the pitch.

The luncheon members seem pleased with this inside explanation but they have some questions.

"Why didn't you pass more?"

Paterno handles this familiar question with a familiar reply. "Because the ground game was going so well. Why put the ball up in the air?"

"Why did you try that kickoff on the ground?" someone asks.

"Because of the bad wind," Paterno says. "We didn't want to put it up there where the wind might hold it up. We thought we could do better by kicking it along the ground."

Paterno is used to the second-guessing. It is the joy of every Monday-morning quarterback to be able to question the coach's judgment on the previous Saturday. Since Paterno calls all the plays, sending them in by rotating his flanker back, he is expected to do all the explaining. And take all the blame for calls that fail.

A questioner wants to know why, with a fourth down and short yardage near the goal line, Paterno had called on the tailback again to carry the ball. "Everyone in the stadium knew it was coming—he'd been carrying the ball all afternoon."

Paterno is irritated, but patient in his reply. There are reasons behind a decision during a game that only a coach can feel. They are not always easily explained after they are made.

"We did score," he says. "I felt at that point that if we were going to go down the drain, we would go down with our best. He had a hot hand. He was a little reckless. He was faster and hitting harder. I'm afraid I can't tell you why. After spending over twenty years on the sidelines, you go with a certain call you know is right."

5 | STRETCH, TEACH, THUD

W HILE PATERNO is talking to the large gathering of luncheon "quarterbacks" at the Inn, preparations for Saturday continue without stop in the coaches' offices at the nearby Rec Hall. It is a time when players drop by after morning study or exams to go over the films. Two of the Hero linebackers have asked Frank Patrick to let them see the opponents' offense. As they watch the action on the screen he keeps up a steady call of questions:

"Now we're in 50 Rotate. Where do you line up?"

"Head on with the tackle," one of them says.

"Right."

"You go where?"

"Inside."

"That's it!"

The opponents' game on the screen and Coach Patrick's questions to the Heroes on alignment and reaction go on for forty-five minutes.

Some of the option plays are run and rerun four or five times. At Penn State the effort is to overcoach the problems. It is, they feel, the best way to get the players to overcome them before Saturday.

S HORTLY AFTER three that afternoon the linebackers are seated on tables in the training quarters while trainers tape their ankles for practice. Since neither of them requires any special taping attention, the job is done quickly by the expert hands. One of them has Coach Jerry Sandusky's instruction sheet, titled "Heroes vs. Opponents." But the conversation across the taping tables is about exam schedules. The team's first-string quarterback has a final on Saturday morning, just four hours before he will call the first play of the game. He's glad Friday is a free day, no practice, and he can spend the time preparing for the exam.

At 4:15 the Hero linebackers have pulled their blue defense jerseys on over their pads and joined the Backers, Mikes, and Fritzes for a five-minute drill on ball reaction—"intercepting" the quick, short passes thrown by graduate assistants. Then there are eight minutes of rehearsal of defending against the option and the pass when the opponents have twins, a flanker and an end, set wide toward the sidelines.

The coaches' voices cut through the sharp November air: "Bill, you don't have that concentration. Think! Think! Why do we practice all these options?"

The players yell their defensive calls. The foreign team quarterback

Coach Paterno demonstrates blocking point to a tight end and linebackers

When a mistake is made, Paterno or an assistant is quick to see that it is corrected

*During team stretch drill, former quarterback Paterno plays
a little toss and catch*

Every drill during the four days of practice before a game is carefully timed by Paterno

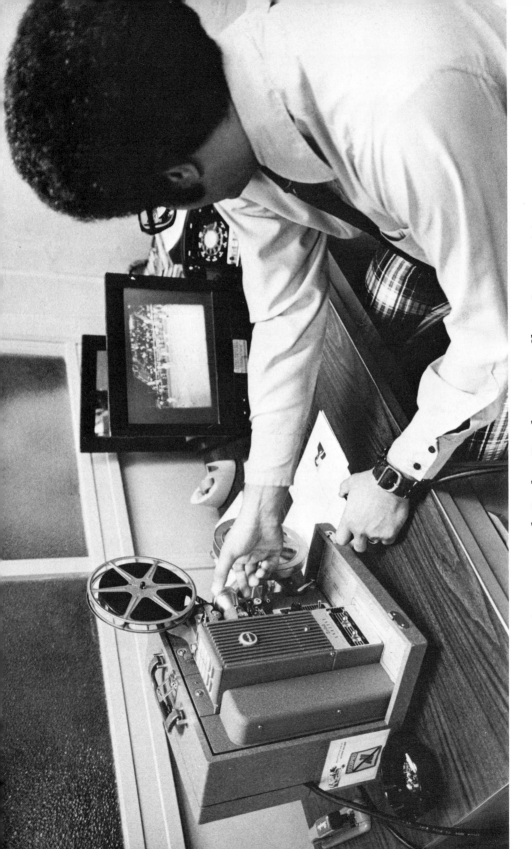

*Assistant coach Booker Brooks reviews films of a promising
high school football player*

Player with a new position goes over his assignment with defensive coach Jim O'Hora

*An offensive lineman does personal study of film showing
Penn State's next opponent*

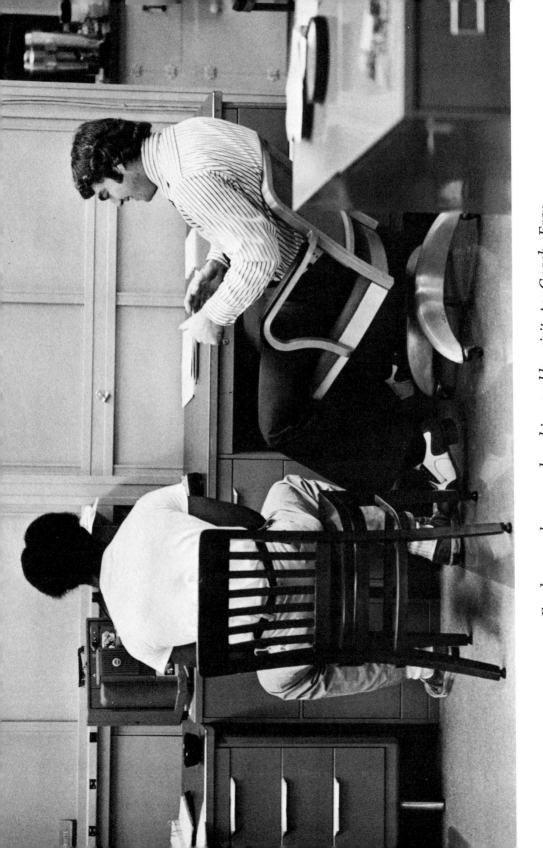

Freshman player makes his weekly visit to Coach Fran Ganter to discuss his classroom work

rifles the ball to his tight end on a rollout pass. As soon as it is completed, the play stops and another begins. Managers hustle fresh footballs to the line of scrimmage so there's no waiting. The action goes swifter than any game.

On the sidelines a pro scout for one of the National Football League teams, who has been attending practice through the week, studies one of the linebackers who is highly rated as a prospect. The scout has been making notes on the linebacker and several other players. This is the eighth university he's visited in the last three weeks. Nowhere has he watched a team practice with the intensity and efficiency of Penn State. "I see now why you win," he says to one of the trainers.

Paterno calls for the six minutes of Stretch. "Okay, let's have a good one," he yells as the lines form and Jerry Sandusky starts the light exercises. Paterno watches from the edge of the formation, occasionally spiraling a football into the air and catching it. Sometimes the Stretch period will give him a clue about a player's morale; sometimes he can get a feeling of whether the team has been working too hard or not hard enough.

In the individual drills, from 4:34 to 4:40, offensive linemen review their blocks, backs run the ropes and the scoring drill, defensive linemen hit the sled, linebackers and defensive halfbacks practice their keys.

During the twelve minutes of Teach the offense and defense play their game against the opponents. On one field the blue offensive team, Saturday's probable starters, run five basic plays against the foreign defense. One of the plays will be the first one called in the game. At the other end of the field the green-shirted offensive team reviews its goal-line and short-yardage plays against the defenses the opponents are most likely to use in those situations.

Paterno stands in the middle of the field where the red and blue defensive teams work against the opponents' offense. His voice carries to the linebackers and secondary across the line of scrimmage: "Come on, now. No lousy habits!" He watches the foreign team break out of the huddle and move crisply into the opponents' formation. As they were on Tuesday, the foreign teams are sharp. They are hitting hard, helping set the tone for a good practice.

Keeping the freshmen involved in their role is a key part of game preparation. A week ago they were looking forward to their own game against another freshman team and it affected their work. Many of them weren't eager to risk injury by going all-out against the varsity in practice. Their lack of combativeness may have hurt Penn State in last Saturday's game.

As the foreign team runs one of the opponents' sweeps, a freshman back puts a jarring block on a linebacker, jamming his hand with his helmet. The linebacker runs to the sidelines, his hand bleeding and throbbing. It is one of these minor, painful injuries which happen in practice. The linebacker knows he should get out of the lineup immediately, as he would in a game, so that practice won't be interrupted. One of the trainers who are always along the sidelines checks the injury. He places a pad over the small cut. The linebacker holds the hand at shoulder level, waiting for the pain to ease. Within three or four minutes he has taken his position again.

From 5:10 to 5:24 the defense plays against the passing attack. The foreign team mixes draw plays, screens, and fakes with its passes to keep the defense sharp. This is the time when the color calls, which change the defense assignments, get reviewed. It is a practice period that demands all the concentration a defensive player can give it.

Wednesday's Thud drill for the defense is ten quickly run plays during the last eight minutes of practice. It has all the noisy upbeat sounds coaches hope to hear as practice draws to a close. The foreign team breaks from the huddle with a loud hand clap. The defense reacts with spirit. The contact as they converge on the ball carrier is sharp. It is just after 5:50 when the last play is run and the players hit the tackle stick as they head for the locker room.

"Two good nights!" Paterno says. "Maybe we're ready to play."

Now at the end of Wednesday practice much of the heavy work for Saturday is over. Paterno feels at this point the load on the players has been just about right. He's pushed them, but he hasn't lengthened practice. "Work hard while you're at it but don't spend too much time doing it," he says. He has watched other teams play well one week and poorly the next just because they've practiced too hard.

Both the offense and the defense have had two days of playing the game—of doing on the field what the coaches decided by mid-Tuesday would be in the game plan. If there are changes to be made now, the coaches should remove plays or defenses from the game plan. It's hard to eliminate plays during the week but it's usually wise to do so. This week, with many of the players worrying about exams, Paterno is anxious to keep the load as light as possible.

Never add to the game plan late in the week. That's a lesson Paterno learned early as a head coach. Once, before a Penn State–Michigan State game, he put in new pass coverage for the defense on a Friday. When it was used in the game the players were still confused by it.

Paterno's coaching mistake may have been one of the reasons Penn State lost by a big score. "When you're practicing something as late as Friday, you're out of business," he says.

On Wednesdays, Paterno and three of his players go from practice to the University's television studio to appear on the weekly "TV Quarterbacks" show at 7 P.M. The program, which is sent over the state's educational television network, is good promotion for both the football team and the University. The public gets a chance to see and hear some of the student-players who are only numbers to them on Saturday. The viewers also get a chance to send second-guessing questions to Coach Paterno and hear him discuss the film highlights of last Saturday's game.

Under the glare of the studio lights the players of the week—two defensive ends and an offensive guard—are nervous and uncomfortable in their jackets and ties. Both Paterno and the announcer try to put them at ease with questions about their home towns, the courses they're taking, their positions on the team. But the TV camera distracts them. Their replies are brief. They seem more tense than they are on Saturday, sitting on the floor of the dressing room underneath the stadium, waiting for the coaches to send them onto the field.

Finally, the announcer asks the tall defensive end who grew up in Brooklyn what the big difference is between living in the city and in a university town in the middle of the Pennsylvania mountains.

"Well, in Brooklyn the wind whistles through the buildings," he says. "Here at Penn State it whistles right through you."

The remark brings a laugh from everyone. It helps break some of the tension. The players sit back and begin to enjoy listening to their coach handle the questions from the "quarterbacks" in the TV audience. Paterno again must turn back and explain decisions he made on the field four days ago.

"Why didn't you use your receivers more? Why did you play so conservatively?"

"In a game like that you try to control the ball. Ball control comes from your running game. In 67 plays we gained over 400 yards. . . ."

"Why didn't you adjust and do something about stopping their option play at halftime? Don't tell me you did!"

Paterno says, no, they didn't handle the option very well. But the defense has been working hard on it all week. He hopes they'll be able to stop it on Saturday.

"Why didn't you think of using more screen passes?"

Paterno laughs. "You guys out there must be betting on the score of the game. We won, didn't we?"

For Paterno, rest from last week's game, even if it is a big victory, seldom comes easily. The luncheon "quarterbacks," the TV "quarterbacks," the second-guessing fans who write him letters, go on questioning last Saturday's decisions until the next game is played.

He thanks the three players for joining him on the TV show and tells them to get some studying and resting done. He drives back to the Rec Hall to pick up two reels of the opponents' film. He will look at them after a late dinner at home. He may see something he missed earlier in the week.

F O R   M A N Y of the players Wednesday night is a contest between overcoming the aches and weariness of practice and getting their studying done. This week many of them face Thursday exams.

At the fraternity house where he is president, the team's first-string center battles the urge to close his eyes and take a nap. He was up most of the night before preparing a book report for his history course. Tomorrow he has a final in humanities. He's sure he'll have to write an essay using some of the ideas of Aristotle and Plato.

When he was on the freshman team two years earlier, he always seemed to lose the fight to stay awake and study. He went to the library night after night and ended up asleep over his books at the table. Part of it was exhaustion from working with the foreign teams against the varsity. Part of it was because he hurt in so many places. Part of it was discouragement. He was moved from position to position in the line. He wanted to quit, but he stuck it out when he saw that many other freshman players felt they didn't fit in either.

Now he looks forward to Saturday and facing the challenge across the line from a tough opponent. He takes so much pride in being on the team he would be there even without a scholarship. It didn't come easily—but the game is now fun. That's what Paterno tells them it should be.

6 | TIME TO STAY READY

"W<small>E'RE NOT</small> going to work very much today," Paterno tells his coaches. "We've had two good sessions. They're getting a little tired. We don't want to leave the game out there."

The final practice of the week will last only one hour and five minutes. The tempo has eased but the game preparation goes on all day, in one form or another, for both coaches and players.

It is a Thursday-morning ritual before home games to check the list of players who will go by bus to Lewistown, some thirty miles away, to spend Friday night at a motel. The night away from the campus brings the team together for more relaxation and sleep than they would get at the University dorms and fraternity houses. The travel list is kept on one wall of the coaches' meeting room. The names are hidden behind a curtain bearing the words "Eastern Champions," with the years in which Penn State won the title. When the curtain is pulled the coaches check the names listed under each position—Pass

End, Left Tackle, Fritz, Mike, Hero, Safety, etc. There are fifty-two names on the travel list.

Before going into the day's work schedule Paterno is anxious to take care of some end-of-semester problems. He passes out a stack of cards showing each player's exam schedule. He knows that exams will conflict with practice for the next several days. When, he wonders, is the best possible time to schedule practice?

"What! Psychology at four o'clock," he grumbles, when he's told several of the players have late exams Monday. "I wonder if they have this problem at Alabama."

Exams will end the day before Thanksgiving. Paterno wants to make sure the players know they'll have Thanksgiving dinner together on the Thursday before the next game. "They can invite parents, wives, children, fiancées. But tell them the girls have to be fiancées," he says with a laugh.

A secretary interrupts to ask if Coach Booker Brooks can take a long-distance call from Cleveland.

"It's the high school coach," Booker says. "He'll want to know if I've seen the film."

"How does he look?" Paterno asks.

"He's a good-looking boy," Booker says.

The call is one of an increasing number which Brooks gets at this time of year. They come from high school coaches who have sent films of their leading players so that Penn State can scout them. Some of the films are requested by Penn State; others come with a recommendation from a coach or perhaps a Penn State alumnus. High school prospects are watched throughout the fall by State coaches and the assistant athletic director. November is the time to decide which players should be contacted and which should be offered scholarships.

"Okay, let's talk about Saturday," Paterno says after rearranging next week's practice time.

Coach John Chuckran begins by reading the eleven names on the kickoff team who will start the game. Then he lists the backups.

Paterno stops him at one of the names, a back with limited experience on the kickoff team. "Did he pick it up all right?"

"Yes, he was in there," Chuckran says. The way the substitute ran and blocked had been given particular attention.

The lineups for the other special teams—extra points and field goals —are reviewed. They will get a chance to practice their specialty for a few minutes in the afternoon.

"What should we open with?" Paterno asks. He now wants to get a feeling from the offensive coaches of how they would set the early pattern for the game. The exchange this morning will help him with some first decisions on Saturday.

"I think a pass. A strong right Pass 32," Booker Brooks says. "In their last game they [the opponents] played mostly zone."

"I'd start with a G Automatic. Then the 45 Draw," says coach of the backs Bob Phillips.

"What would you do on pass down?" Paterno asks.

"With third down and eight, I'd use the B Fly."

"What about Pass 31?" Paterno questions.

"I like the B Fly," Phillips says. "We've been hitting the right man all week in practice."

"We run the G Automatic so well," says Dick Anderson.

"82's a good pass for us."

"Correct me," Paterno says, "but wouldn't the X back pattern to the sideline be open? They give very little roll. . . ."

"Their big 83 just doesn't get back at all."

The defensive coaches get their turn to play the game.

"If you have only three defenses what would you use?" Paterno asks.

"50 Rotate, Fritz Blow, State Blow," Frank Patrick says.

"The State Blitz has looked very good," Jim O'Hora says. "I like that, the 8 Rotate, and the 6 Blow."

Paterno reaches for a piece of chalk. One more time he wants to see a potential defensive problem in Xs and Os. "The hard baby is if their tackle comes at us a little to the inside and beats our man. . . ." At some point early in the game on Saturday he will probably find out from his spotters in the press box if the problem is a real one.

J. T. White thinks the 8 Rotate with an overshift, the 6 Tough under-shift, and the 6 Blow will work best against the opponents' basic attack.

Paterno offers his choices. "I'd start with the 8 Rotate," he says, "and mix with the 6 Blow. If we get a game we don't expect from them, then go to the Fritz Blow."

The talk turns back to the offense.

"I really don't want to start the game with an automatic," Paterno says. "We'll be anxious to get going out there. I don't want the easy yards early. Two weeks ago [when Penn State scored two touchdowns in the first five minutes of the game] I felt very uneasy. We had all those points and we hadn't punished anyone.

"Those teams that want to pass early—and keep passing. They're throwing the ball and they're not punching. They're not hitting."

Paterno wants to know if the new pattern they have added to Pass 82—to take advantage of the slow reactions of one of the opponents' defensive backs—looks okay in practice.

"Good," he says, when told that it's been put in. "We'll call it 82 Go." It is the one new pass play that Penn State has added for the game.

"All right. Is there anything you've seen in practice that you don't like?" Paterno wants to know.

"I wouldn't run any counters," Bob Phillips says.

Paterno wonders if the ball handling on the counter plays has gone badly during practice.

"No, that's not it." But the counter plays haven't fooled one of the big freshman linemen who plays defense on the foreign team.

"I'm not sure you can fool him," Paterno says. He's a freshman who has made a strong impression against the varsity lately.

During the break in the coaches' meeting Booker Brooks goes back to his desk and to a film on a prospect from a New Jersey high school. The player is a wide receiver and Brooks will begin by judging his speed, moves, and aggressiveness on the basis of the film made at a high school night game a few weeks before.

At the far end of the coaches' office Fran Ganter sits in conference with a freshman player. All freshmen on the team are required to visit Fran once a week during the season and discuss their academic program. He serves as a guidance counselor to freshmen, making sure they're keeping up their credits and aren't having too much trouble with any particular course. Players may want to know what sections of a course they should try to get into, which instructors and professors are considered the best. The guidance effort is one reason over 90 percent of the football players at Penn State graduate on time. They don't end up as seniors with too few credits to finish with their class.

Because he has been busy with term papers and final exams, the offensive co-captain has had to wait until Thursday for his personal review of the opponents' films. He and the other first-string guard like to get to the coaches' office to study the films together by Wednesday. But he is at the projector alone this morning. Yesterday's hard practice and his studies in business administration sent him to bed at 11:30 last night. He wants to see the film before going back to his books.

As an offensive guard he carefully checks to see how the man across the line plays the pass block. Does he hit quickly or does he lay back a little? On the pass rush, does he grab? Does he come right at you?

The opponents try a blitz on the screen, and the co-captain watches this segment several times. He notices one move by the defense that might warn him the blitz is coming. The safety man moves up a little to fill in for the linebacker. It seems clear enough on the film taken from the top of the stadium. But from his position at left guard he won't be able to see the move very well. He talks to John Chuckran about it. Would it be possible to get a signal, maybe from the quarterback, to tell him the safety man is filling in?

Paterno stops to watch the film briefly and to talk with the co-captain. The four captains often come to Paterno on behalf of the team, bringing complaints about the food at the training table or other problems. Paterno likes to check with them on team morale. What do they think the general attitude is about the coming game? It's a way of letting them know he cares how they feel.

The co-captain says it's been a hard practice week. He thinks everyone's blood is boiling for Saturday's game. "No one is taking them lightly," he says. "We know they come from a tough conference."

Paterno hopes that at this point there is a lot of determination and no overconfidence. "Once you get to the place during practice where you think you can't lose," he says, "that's the week it's going to happen."

When Paterno returns to his own office he has to deal with an off-the-field problem, the kind of thing every coach must handle every so often. At a recent rock concert there had been a scuffle around the entrance between students and local youths. One of the locals had been slightly injured and had decided to press charges against the student who hit him, a member of the freshman team. Paterno is told the freshman must appear before the Justice of the Peace. He decides it would be better for the player and the team if he dropped off the squad until the legal matter is cleared up. Paterno and the player will talk after he has faced the local justice.

As T H E players report for Thursday practice, on a day of high warm wind and threatening rain, there is no doubt about the tempo. It was set during the hard workouts of Tuesday and Wednesday. "You know what you're going to do on Saturday and how to do it," one of the seniors says. "From now on it's a matter of staying ready."

The tailback who felt so leg-heavy on Tuesday is getting his bounce back. He's forgotten about the bruises that required four cold packs after last Saturday's game.

The sophomore safety man no longer worries about the difference in the angle of his body when the defense is 6 Blow instead of 6 Tough. Frank Patrick has hammered away at the problem all week. It is finally getting automatic for him.

The pass end who was so discouraged on Tuesday about the way he was playing the option has more confidence about holding his own. Again this afternoon Paterno will be working with him and the other ends in the early minutes of practice.

To help his offensive linemen stay ready, John Chuckran gives them a handwritten sheet of reminders and pointers for the game. It begins: "I know that you are not underestimating the opponents because of the way you have practiced this week. They will be tough because they will be trying to prove a point.

"We are improving on our takeoffs and our hitting has become crisper. Let's continue to improve."

Chuckran has listed ten points he wants his guards and centers to keep in mind. The first is on technique: "On the bump technique, be sure you are low enough. Aim your head for the far knee of the nose-man [middle guard]."

The list ends with the reminder of a signal change: "When 0 Sweep (8 Sweep) is called in the huddle: If the quarterback calls '0–0' or '0–8' at the line, the sweep is off and the play now becomes 0 Swap or 8 Swap. Good luck!"

Chuckran's weekly reminders are another way of keeping the interior linemen alert as the game practice comes to a close. Of all the players on the team they appear to have the most tedious jobs. They spend much of their time working on blocking assignments on small pieces of ground. This week practice has been made more challenging because the foreign teams have given them a hard, sharp look at the opponents' defense.

Thursday practice, like all the rest, is run full speed, but without shoulder pads. Paterno takes the ends and Fritz linebackers for the first ten minutes for one more round of reaction to the option play. The players are more alert, more confident than they were early in the week. He lets them know they're better.

"Good! John. Good position. That's it!

"That's right. Stay in there until you see that ball pitched and then down the line!

"No, don't do a dance. Just hold. Good. Good!"

After three days of talking and drilling their execution is right. They won't make mistakes again on Saturday if they concentrate as they are this afternoon.

Practice is without the hard individual work of Tuesday and Wednesday—without the fall-on-ball drill, the sled, the quick bags, the goal-line tackling. It's more of a dress rehearsal for Saturday.

The defense reviews its coverage of kicks and kickoffs. The team's kickers and centers practice their carefully coordinated effort in the kicking game. Coach Patrick checks the timing with a stopwatch. He wants to make sure the kick is off fast enough after the pass from center. He wants the ball up in the air long enough so that it can be well covered.

The offense spends twelve minutes sharpening its takeoffs on a series of plays against the opponents' defense, with the freshmen holding the familiar shields. The sweeps, draw plays, pitchouts, screen passes, special shifts, trap plays, all get a spirited review.

As Paterno whistles at 4:48, sending them into the final period of practice, there are jokes at the portable water cooler. "Hey, it's beer tonight!" one sweating lineman yells. "Thursday's good—but Friday's better."

The offensive guard whose strained ankle ligaments kept him on crutches at practice earlier in the week, joins teammates as they grab a quick drink at the water cooler. He is off crutches but still in street clothes. He won't even dress for the game on Saturday but he'll be on the sidelines, very much a part of the team. He is already thinking ahead to next week's game, his last as a senior. He wants to be sure he can help win that one.

The concluding twelve plays of Thud by the offense go faster than usual. The last is a quick rehearsal of a two-point conversion play, just in case it's needed in a close game on Saturday.

Paterno sends them in with the words "Stay off your feet as much as possible. I know you've got exams. But take it easy!"

The senior tackle is the last player through the gate. His step seems to be lighter tonight.

Inside the training quarters the noise level is up everywhere. The coaches' locker room is livelier than on any other night during the week. Thursday is special for them too. It is "Coaches' Night Out," a night when they all get together with their wives for dinner at a State College restaurant. It is an evening to relax and talk about families. And more football.

7 | "LET'S HAVE A GOOD BALL GAME"

L ESS THAN twenty-four hours before he will be dressing for the game the freshman defensive tackle uneasily enters the coaches' offices at Rec Hall. He is worried about final exams, the first he's ever taken at the University. But now, late Friday morning, he is even more concerned about football and all of the things he must keep in his head for the game tomorrow.

He is one of two freshmen who have been working with the varsity during the week. The promotion is a result of injuries at the position. But he has earned it. His name and number are on the depth chart, which means he is one of the sixty players most likely to be used on offense or defense. Even though he won't be starting, and may not play at all, he must prepare as if he were. In the line he would be taking a position next to the defensive co-captain, a senior and an All-American candidate and one of the best players on the team.

Coach Jim O'Hora has asked him to come in and review his assignments. They will go over the basic defenses, the way he lines up, his moves, the color calls that change his assignment. Although he has studied the play book all fall and this week's defensive game plan, even some of the terms still bother him.

He sits hunched closely to O'Hora at his desk as they discuss the defenses written on separate cards. "Now on the State Blitz," O'Hora says patiently, "if you get lined up properly, your outside foot is on the inside foot of the tackle. An adjustment comes if the formation is right and you are away. Away from the formation, that is. You line up on the shoulder so that he has to work on you. If he doesn't, you're free!

"On 6 Tough you're the long man. You just hit target areas on 6 Tough.

"Try to think in terms of alignment first. When you hear 50s, 8s, or 6s you see the defense right away. You shouldn't have to think about it.

"We say 6 Blow, think alignment. Where do you line up? You do what?"

"Blitz to the tight-end side."

"All right. On the 6 Blow, who dictates the blitz? The tight end.

"Remember, it all starts with alignment. Then you separate those things that don't take you on straight-ahead action.

"Now, they go into a quick lineup and you get a gray call. What does it mean? Check that game plan again because the color is gray this week. It means you switch to the 6 Blow."

"The trouble is," the freshman says, "I have to think and then do it. That puts me a step behind. I'm thinking behind them."

"We can't play without these details," O'Hora says. "They don't come easily. A lot of guys are depending upon you to do your job out there. Take some time today and do some thinking in your room. I've grouped the defenses together on these cards. Think of them in their categories. See how they're related. We can talk about them again tonight."

The freshman takes the cards and heads back to his dormitory room. It was less than three months ago, when he first reported to the freshman team, that he felt overwhelmed by the details of playing defense. He couldn't believe it when he learned there was a difference between lining up on the nose or the eye of the man opposite! He learned that on a blitz if he took one step to the inside he had made a costly mental error. He knew he was big and fast enough. He enjoyed the hitting. But the mental side of the job has taken much longer than he thought it would. The defensive game plan seems more than enough to keep in his head. He wishes he were a junior or senior and the knowledge was all stored away.

T HE COACHES' gathering on Friday is shorter than most. It is a time for late discussion of the team's mental fitness. And Paterno wants to pin down decisions on how they will start playing the game.

"How do you think they felt after practice?" he asks.

The coaches agree that practice went well. There were some mental errors. A second-string back ran a wrong pattern on a familiar pass play. One of the ends is still too eager playing the option. Not everyone gave a hundred percent on the two kickoffs.

"I want to use 8 Rotate, 50 Rotate, and 6 Blow," Paterno says. "Let's see if we can handle them with that.

"I'd start the ball game with the 46 Draw," he adds.

"If they run a blow at us," one of the defensive coaches says, "and they stack away from the formation, we're minus an end."

"We'll run it to the formation."

"That Pass 30," an offensive coach says, "we're now throwing it as well as we have all season."

Paterno wants to talk about the game assignments for the coaches. They discuss who will be upstairs in the press box, who will handle the phones along the sidelines. As always, Paterno will be sending in the plays; O'Hora will be signaling changes in defense.

All of the coaches have another brief pre-game duty tomorrow. A group of high school senior football players will attend the game with their families or friends. The coaches will meet these prospects at a buffet at eleven o'clock in Rec Hall. It is all part of the other side of a coach's job—recruiting. National signing day, when all universities announce the names of players who have agreed to football scholarships, is still three months away. But the search for next year's freshman players is at a peak. As soon as the season ends, most of the Penn State coaches will be on the road contacting the players they want to enroll at the University.

On this Friday, Paterno turns the end of the meeting over to a discussion of prospects, some of whom they will meet for the first time tomorrow.

The assistant athletic director in charge of recruiting student-athletes, Sever Toretti, sits with the coaches and reviews the list. The high school players are rated according to ability, attitude, and scholarship. At Penn State a player's ability to get by in the classroom is highly important.

Toretti goes over the names, with short descriptions of each player's strengths and weaknesses. If Fran Ganter or Booker Brooks or anyone else has been able to scout the player on film or in person, their opinions are added. The list is long. Only a few will get scholarship offers. Paterno will eventually interview all of the selected players.

"As a back he's rated high in Maryland, despite his size," Toretti begins. "But he's a marginal student. . . .

"He's been at the prep school for three years," he says of another prospect. "He must be an excellent student because his grades are high and the school is tough. His coach suggests he be considered as a tight end. He's been playing fullback all season. . . ."

The talk turns to the outstanding quarterbacks in Pennsylvania high schools. Several of them have been scouted by Penn State.

"Now this boy has good rank in class but his College Boards are hurting him. . . ."

"The only fault I saw," Booker says of a quarterback he has watched on film, "is he throws the ball from up here." He indicates an awkward, overhead motion.

The quarterback review focuses on two names. Paterno says, "We agree that everything is good about both of them. I think we should go ahead. Let's talk to them. The sign-up deadline is March 6. That's a lot sooner than you think."

At noon Booker Brooks says he must leave for the airport. He is off to scout next week's opponent and bring back more film on Sunday.

"Good luck," he says to his fellow coaches.

Friday afternoon in the coaches' offices is turned over to details which don't always involve tomorrow's game. There are phone calls to be returned, invitations to high school football banquets to accept, game tickets and visitors to handle. There are always last-minute points to make to the players, and they should be taken care of tonight or early tomorrow in the dressing room. Bob Phillips prepares for a last meeting with the quarterbacks. Friday afternoon remains an odd piece of time. It is too late to worry about how practice is going; it is too early to give in to that edgy pre-game feeling.

Penn State used to take a light workout on the field on Fridays, whether the game was at home or away. When the team was traveling, the warmup drill was followed by a bus trip to the airport and a flight to the site of the game. Friday could be a busy day of preparing, dressing, packing, and travel. Paterno decided that the small amount of running and loosening up in the workout took too much time, that it added little to the preparation for the game. If the team isn't ready to play by the end of Thursday's workout, it won't be ready at all. The decision to drop the Friday warmup was most welcome to the players. "It's best," one of them said, "to wake up on Friday and feel you've earned the day off."

AT EIGHT o'clock on Friday, as punctually as they take the field for a midweek practice, the players file into the bus in front of Rec Hall for the ride to Lewistown. To the seniors on the team the Friday-night trip to the motel away from the campus is as much a part of the pre-game pattern as lacing up their shoes in the locker room on Saturday morning. Some of them carry books for exam study; others have the special game instructions for their position in their pockets. Most of them are beginning to get the taste of anticipation which will grow stronger as the game approaches.

The coaches follow the team over the mountain to Lewistown in the University van or private cars. One coach, a team trainer, and a manager will stay overnight at the motel; the others will return to State College. Paterno rides in the van, having spent the last hour and a half at a gathering of sportswriters who will be covering tomorrow's game. The informal press party each Friday evening gives the out-of-town writers and radio-TV reporters a chance to meet Paterno and ask questions about the game and the team. Paterno enjoys the opportunity to relax and exchange opinions on everything from international politics to the probable weather for the game.

At the motel the fifty-two players are paired in rooms according to position. Flankers together, tailbacks together, safety men together. The Friday night away from the distractions of the campus adds just a little more to the team feeling, acquired by working hard together and playing together the last several months. Each Friday night the players are reminded they are part of one unit that will take the field tomorrow. They will win or lose together.

Paterno has said: "I think this is something people really don't understand about team sports. They don't quite get it. But those of us who are close to it can see it. When you look at your team praying together before a game you can actually feel their love, respect, and admiration for each other. Here are people who have lost their individuality and subordinated their personal interest to whatever is for the good of the team. They want to do well so their team can win. They don't care about how much publicity they are going to get. As a coach, you know when they go out on the field with that much love and respect for one another—this losing themselves in something they think is a little bigger than they are—they will be tough to beat."

At the motel the players go directly to a small meeting room off the main lobby. On a table there is a light snack for each—a sandwich, an apple, a carton of milk. Most of them will add to the ration by getting candy out of the machines in the lobby on their way to their rooms. The players take seats in rows of folding chairs for a Friday-night tradition—the team raffle. The prize may be no more than a flashy sports shirt but the game is rich with laughs. It helps loosen things up.

Paterno says a few words before sending them off to their rooms. It is as much of a "pep talk" as he will give before the game.

"You've done well this week and worked hard," he tells them. "You've worked hard together since the beginning of practice last spring. And it's been a long season. I know you're not going to let the goals you've worked for slip away by taking them too lightly tomorrow. You know how much they want to beat you. You've got the right attitude. You've got pride in what you've accomplished. Tomorrow let's go out and have fun. Let's have a good ball game."

That's all. The meeting ends and the players hurry to their rooms. The assistant coaches make their rounds, stopping long enough at each room to make sure things are all right, to ask or answer questions about the game. Coach O'Hora takes extra time with the freshman tackle, quizzing him again about his alignment in a half-dozen defenses. He has the answers but he has to stop and think about them. He knows he's taking longer than he'll have time for tomorrow.

Trainer Chuck Medlar, who will stay at the motel, checks those players who need treatment before they go to sleep. He begins his rounds by applying heat to the sore shoulder of the second-string fullback. He makes sure the defensive starter with the back problem has a bedboard for the night.

In their room two of the Hero linebackers take one more look at Jerry Sandusky's written game instruction. They have had a good practice week. They have all but forgotten about last week's game and the lane they left open that let the opponents gain so much ground on the option. Neither of them can remember a tougher talk than Paterno gave them on Tuesday. Or a harder practice. They have been "up" and ready to play ever since.

In other rooms the TV sets are switched on. They will stay on until lights-out at eleven. Several of the players must be up early enough to take the van back to the campus in time for eight-o'clock exams or early Mass. Most of the players will go to church sometime in the morning.

As the coaches gather at the motel entrance to share rides home, the snow that has been threatening during the week of practice begins to fall. The team they are leaving behind in the motel is as well prepared as possible. They are ready to play their game. A little snow won't matter.

8 | LAST WORDS

Each saturday game remains a fresh challenge to Paterno, a testing of himself and of the job he and the other coaches have done during the previous six days. Will the team play even a little harder than they have been pushed this week? Will they hold on to their poise? Will the quarterback, who spent the morning on a final exam, find his passing rhythm? Will the team stay strong through the last play of the game?

These are questions that make the approach to Saturday exciting. Paterno looks forward to being part of the test. He enjoys making decisions on the sidelines. He likes the feeling of his players around him, the flow of movement on the field, the crowd noise. Each game is the same and yet very different.

The hours leading up to the game—the end of six days of preparation—fit into a familiar pattern for him. They bring a steady rise in the emotions for coaches and players alike. At midmorning the team gathers in a private dining room at the Inn for the pre-game meal. It is a traditional meal of steak and eggs and pancakes and bacon. More meal than they really need. He and the other coaches sit outside the dining room at a separate table, drinking coffee. The talk is casual, familiar. But even veteran coach Jim O'Hora can't conceal the feeling of tension. It is something they share with the players.

The players eat rapidly, leaving one who always finishes last because he chews so carefully. The coaches wait until he has finished before walking to nearby Rec Hall to meet with the high school players and the other guests. Paterno talks with as many of them as he can before he has to leave for the dressing room and the game.

Paterno always takes this walk through the campus alone. It is about a mile from Rec Hall to the training quarters near the stadium. It is his only chance before the game to do some private thinking. Along the way students greet him, but he tries to hold to a steady walking pace. He knows how he wants to start the game, how he wants to play the game. But he must wait until after the kickoff to find out if the team can play the game they have planned.

When he enters the training quarters he finds an atmosphere of calm edged with tension. It is like this every Saturday morning. The trainers swiftly, expertly taping. The players with an outward look of ease on the tables. A few early dressers in their bright white game pants seated around a table playing Crazy Eights. Jerry Sandusky at a small blackboard talking to a reserve linebacker: "Now on State Cross you're always away from the formation. . . ."

The players and coaches take buses from the training quarters to the stadium, inching their way through the crowds hurrying to the entrance gates. Underneath the stadium the people yell and clap as the players unload in front of the dressing room. There is the wait before it is time to go out for the pre-game warmup, which temporarily unties some of the knots in the stomach. When everyone is back from the field

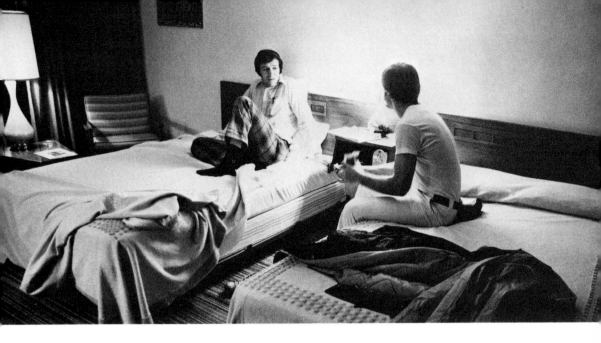

On Friday night, two Penn State linebackers talk about the game at motel where team stays

Paterno greets parents of high school prospects who have come to watch Penn State play

*Two hours before game time, Paterno walks alone through
the campus to team's dressing quarters*

In crowded locker room under the stadium, Paterno and players wait to take the field

Paterno gives a quiet, low-key talk to players. "Let's have a good ball game," he says

Before each game, the players and coaches repeat the Lord's Prayer together

On their way to the field, Penn State players pass beneath fans on the stadium ramps

Paterno and assistants walk between rows of players during the pre-game exercises

On the sidelines, Paterno and assistants finally learn how well they have prepared during the week

and in the dressing room, they quickly get off their feet. Some players sit with their backs to the concrete walls; others lie on the floor with their heads propped up on their helmets. Paterno quietly discusses signal cadence with his starting quarterback. He suggests that they try to run off plays more rapidly when the wind is behind them and slow it down a little against the wind.

An offensive co-captain asks, "Joe, do you want the ball or the wind?" Paterno says he'll make that coin-tossing decision when they go out again.

Short minutes before they are to take the field, Paterno says, familiarly, "Okay, fellows, let's go." Everyone is up. "Let's have a good ball game!" The players are pressed around him, helmets in their hands. "We'll say our prayer," Paterno adds. The players kneel as one and, in cadenced voices, repeat "The Lord's Prayer."

It's time to turn the dressing room over to the captains of the team. The coaches step outside and close the door. These last words before game time belong to the players.